诸子百家国风画传

The Pictorial Biographies of Great Thinkers

庄子

画传

图 / 赵明钧
文 / 海连
译 / 秦悦

ZHUANGZI

济南出版社

图书在版编目（CIP）数据

庄子画传 / 赵明钧著． -- 济南 ：济南出版社,2015.4（诸子百
家国风画传）（2017.4 重印）
ISBN 978-7-5488-1532-7

Ⅰ．①庄… Ⅱ．①赵… Ⅲ．①庄周(约前369～前286)－传记－
画册 Ⅳ．① B223.5-64

中国版本图书馆 CIP 数据核字 (2015) 第 070446 号

◆图 / 赵明钧　◆文 / 海连　◆译 / 秦悦

◎"原动力"中国原创动漫出版扶持计划入选项目
◎上海市重大文艺创作项目由上海文化发展基金会资助
◎上海市文化"走出去"项目由上海市文化"走出去"专项扶持资金赞助

庄子画传

出版发行	济南出版社
总 执 行	上海海派连环画中心
	上海城市动漫出版传媒有限公司
	济南出版有限责任公司
项目策划	刘 军　刘亚军
出版策划	崔 刚　朱孔宝
出版执行	张承军
责任编辑	胡长娟　张雪丽
特约编辑	刘蓉蓉　孙羽翎　余 阳　路艳艳
装帧设计	舒晓春　焦萍萍

印 刷	济南鲁艺彩印有限公司
开 本	210mm×285mm　　16 开
印 张	5.75
字 数	90 千
版 次	2015 年 4 月第 1 版
印 次	2017 年 4 月第 2 次印刷
标准书号	ISBN 978-7-5488-1532-7
定 价	45.00 元

庄子画传 ZHUANGZI

前言

2014年3月，中国国家主席习近平在联合国教科文组织总部的演讲中指出：「中华文明经历了五千多年的历史变迁，但始终一脉相承，积淀着中华民族最深层的精神追求，代表着中华民族独特的精神标识，为中华民族生生不息、发展壮大提供了丰厚滋养。」中华传统文化是潺潺流水，润物无声，滋养了世代中国人的精神家园。在中华传统文化波澜壮阔的历史画卷中，诸子百家文化就是其中浓墨重彩的一页。

充满先贤智慧的诸子百家文化，是集中华传统文化、哲学、艺术于一体的文明宝藏：反对暴力，期盼人与人之间和睦相处、以礼相待，这是儒家思想的「仁」；平等博爱，止息不义战争，这是墨家思想的「兼爱非攻」；遵循自然、万物和谐，这是道家思想的「道法自然」；论兵却主张「不战而屈人之兵」，这是充满智慧光芒的兵家思想……诸子百家的思想，正包含着人们所努力构造的幸福世界中的重要基石。这是中华民族的财富，也是世界文明的重要组成部分。

近代以来，上海作为中华文明走向世界的一个重要窗口，担当着向世界展示中国文化华彩精粹的重要使命。建设充满活力的国际文化大都市，上海更需要放眼全球、放眼全国，以「海纳百川」的精神打造中华文化精品，推动中华文化走向世界。

这套由国务院新闻办公室发起，上海市政府新闻办公室、山东省政府新闻办公室、河南省政府新闻办公室协力出版的《诸子百家国风画传》丛书，化繁难为轻逸、化艰深为平易，充满了思想美、故事美、人性美、艺术美。它将诸子思想中的妙笔华章与国画家的水墨丹青巧妙结合，书香墨趣将诸子的音容笑貌、神采风骨生动地呈现在读者面前。它向世界打开了中华传统文化之门，同时也为中华文化拓展国际文化交流，进行了新的尝试和创新，提供了新的载体和通道。

诸子百家文化精神正如追逐理性、自由与美的古希腊人文精神一般，是人类共同的文化财富。希望诸位读者从这套书出发，分享故事，体验艺术，感悟哲理，开始一段美不胜收的中华传统文化探源之旅。

灿如云霞的中华文化让世人心向往之。

二〇一四年九月

Preface

In March of 2014, President Xi Jinping pointed out in his speech delivered in the headquarters of UNESCO, "Having gone through over 5000 years of vicissitudes, the Chinese civilization has always kept to its original root. Unique in representing China spiritually, it contains some most profound pursuits of the Chinese nation and provides it with abundant nourishment for existence and development." The Chinese traditional culture is just like trickling water irrigating and nurturing the spiritual realm of Chinese people. In the long and splendid picture of Chinese cultural history, the contributions of great thinkers are the most glorious chapter.

The wisdom and philosophies of these great thinkers crystallized culture, philosophy and art in our Chinese civilization: Confucian "benevolence", Mohist "universal love", Taoist "modeling itself after Nature" and the military teaching about "attaining victory in war without fighting" are still holding the stage. These fascinating thoughts constitute the cornerstones of an ideal world that Chinese people dream of having. These spiritual assets not only belong to Chinese people but also constitute an integral part of the world civilization.

As an important window in modern times, Shanghai has assumed a mission to demonstrate the brilliance of Chinese culture. To construct a dynamic international cultural metropolis and to promote Chinese culture to the world, Shanghai needs a mind so open to the entire country and entire world and a mind so tolerant as the vast ocean admitting hundreds of rivers.

The Pictorial Biographies of Great Thinkers supported by The State Council Information Office and Information Office of Shanghai Municipality is a close cooperation between Information Office of Shandong Provincial People's Government and Information Office of Henan Provincial People's Government. This series in Chinese painting style simplified the complicated history into simple stories, revealing the beauty of human nature as well as artistic creation. The ink painting presented vividly the personalities of great thinkers, attracting readers to explore their great thoughts and ideas. The pictorial biographies helped open the door of Chinese traditional culture to the world, and this attempt also provided a new carrier and channel for cultural exchange.

The brilliant Chinese culture is fascinating. Like the pursuit for reason, freedom and beauty in ancient Greek humanism, the legacy from these great thinkers is also the cultural assets shared by the whole humanity. It is hoped that readers can embark on a journey to explore traditional Chinese culture through reading these books.

September 2014

庄子画传 ZHUANGZI

编者的话

战国时期，道家思想的代表人物庄子，一生都过着朴素艰苦的隐世生活。让人惊叹的是，在清贫的物质生活背后，他创造了极其丰富、浪漫的精神世界。庄子极擅用艺术形象来阐明其哲学思想。在庄子的精神世界中，人可以与蝴蝶相互转化，可以与鬼神对话，可以从光怪陆离的景象中参悟出哲理。《庄子画传》从庄子的日常生活写起，让读者对庄子的思想形成独特的管窥门径。画家赵明钧有着丰富的连环画和国画功底，十分讲究色彩和线条的运用。他对庄子精神世界图景的展现多采用鲜明的色彩，而描绘庄子本人时则多采用灰暗的颜色，以示其质朴的生活，让想象与现实形成饶有意味的对比。庄子个性洒脱，语言诙谐幽默，本书为了突出这一特点，人物往往配以夸张而不失趣味的动作，韵味十足。画家还勾勒了种种神怪鸟兽，在水墨画深浅交错的飘逸意境中，引领读者开启前往庄子世界的『奇幻』之旅。

Editor's Note

As a representative figure of Taoism during the Warring States Period, Zhuangzi lived quite a simple life. While comparing with his poverty and hardship, Zhuangzi created a rich and romantic spiritual world. Zhuangzi was extremely good at conveying his philosophical ideas through some artistic images. In his spiritual world, man can become a butterfly, and he can talk with ghost. His message is delivered through this weird, impossible world. *Zhuangzi* lets readers get to know his ideas through his daily life. The artist Zhao Mingjun has a solid foundation and rich experience in picture-story book painting and traditional Chinese painting, and he is very particular about coloring and lines. He highlighted Zhuangzi's spiritual world with bright colors and delineated his simple life with dark colors, thus establishing a sharp contrast between an imagined world and a harsh reality. To represent Zhuangzi's free spirit and humorous language, some portrayals are exaggerated to add fun. The artist also sketched some strange birds and beasts. In his artistic conception with ink, readers can embark on a journey to Zhuangzi's fantasy world.

目录
Contents

《庄子》，亦称《南华经》，道家经典之一，为庄周及其后学的著作集，在哲学、文学方面都具有较高的研究价值。

◎逍遥庄子图
The free and unfettered Zhuangzi

庄子，名周，生卒年、家世、师承渊源，始终都笼罩在历史的迷云中，无法确切知晓。我们只能根据《庄子》《史记》等

古书的记载，大致推测他出生在战国中期的宋国，与魏惠王、齐宣王为同时代人。

Little is known about Zhuangzi, the great thinker named Zhuang Zhou:his birth, his life and his mentors. Everything about Zhuangzi is shrouded in mystery. According to *Zhuangzi* and

Records of the Grand Historian, it is inferred that he was born in the State of Song during the Warring States Period, and he was contemporary with Duke Hui of Wei and Duke Xuan of Qi.

◎庄周梦蝶图
Zhuang Zhou's butterfly dream

天地与我并生，而万物与我为一。（《庄子·齐物论》）

　　战国时期，群雄争霸，诸子百家各创新说。庄子却如同一位遗世而独立的隐者，沉浸在自己的翩翩蝴蝶梦中。他忽而在梦中无拘无束地飞舞，忽而又醒来，分不清究竟是庄子做梦变成了蝴蝶，还是蝴蝶此刻化作了庄子。

　　The Warring States Period witnessed a great number of states competing for hegemony, and hundreds of schools of thoughts contending for attention. However, Zhuangzi, like a recluse, had always kept himself aloof from the competition, and indulged himself in his butterfly dream. He once dreamed that he became a butterfly, fluttering here and there. Suddenly he woke up; but he did not know now whether he was Zhuangzi who dreamed of transforming into a butterfly, or a butterfly that dreamed of transforming into Zhuangzi.

◎离奇梦象图
Strange dreams

方其梦也，不知其梦也。梦之中又占其梦焉，觉而后知其梦也。（《庄子·齐物论》）

在《庄子》一书中，既有高飞九万里的大鹏，也有目光短浅的小鸟；既有在蜗牛角上发生的战斗，也有在海底看管夜明珠的大骊龙。而在诗意的蝴蝶之外，同样也会有亡者的髑髅闯入庄子离奇的梦境。

In *Zhuangzi*, there are stories about a huge bird called Peng soaring as high as 90 thousand *li* in the sky, and a short-sighted small bird; there are also stories about fights on the feelers of a snail, and a dragon looking after a luminous pearl at the bottom of the sea. Apart from the poetic butterfly dream, there are also strange dreams of skulls.

◎路遇髑髅图
Meeting a skull

大知闲闲，小知间间；大言炎炎，小言詹詹。（《庄子·齐物论》）

一天，庄子正去往楚国，见道旁有个髑髅，便上前叩问："您是犯了什么天理，遇上什么祸患，才沦落至此呢？"髑髅不答，庄子竟拉过它来，就地枕着睡着了。

One day, Zhuangzi saw a skull on his way to the State of Chu. He went up and asked, "What made you suffer punishment and lie unburied on the roadside? "The skull said nothing. Zhuangzi then slept with the skull under his head.

◎髑髅托梦图
A skull in dream

去小知而大知明，去善而自善矣。（《庄子·外物》）

　　半夜，髑髅托梦给庄子，说："先生看上去能言善辩，可除饥饿病痛这些生的忧患以外，您对死又有多少了解呢？人世间满布着负累与罪责，生活本身就是一桩苦差。死后的世界，再没有昏庸的君王，也没有欺压百姓的官臣，无所谓四季的轮转，天地是一切的主宰。我终于和生的烦恼做了永诀。你即使拿了王位来，我也不愿交换此刻的轻松与喜悦。"庄子倚靠着髑髅，在黑沉沉的梦里，静听它诉说死后的自在与惬意。

　　In the depth of night, the skull appeared in his dream and said, "Sir, you seem to be eloquent about a lot of things. But besides the concerns such as famine and illness in one's life, how much do you know about death? There are a lot of burdens and guilt one has to live with, and to live is to suffer. In life after death, there are no fatuous kings or cruel ministers. No one cares about the change of seasons, and Heaven and Earth is the master of all. I finally said farewell to these worries. I refuse to trade my peace and joy now for even a crown you offer." Zhuangzi lay against the skull, listening quietly in the dream to what the skull say about the ease and comfort after death.

◎贤人尚志图
A poor but noble Zhuangzi

至人无己，神人无功，圣人无名。（《庄子·逍遥游》）

　　悟透了天道人情的庄子对物质生活不怎么讲究。一次，他身穿打补丁的粗布衣服，脚踏一双用麻绳绑成的旧鞋，就大大方方跑去面见魏惠王。魏惠王问他

为何看上去如此潦倒，庄子却答道："破衣烂鞋，这是贫困；有理想不能施展，才是潦倒。"

　　Zhuangzi did not care much about the material comfort. In rags and worn-out shoes, he went to see Duke Hui of Wei. When Duke Hui asked why he was so frustrated, Zhuangzi answered,

"Tattered clothes and shoes only show one's poverty, but an unfulfilled ideal is what really makes one frustrated."

◎濮水钓鱼图
Zhuangzi fishing

不乐寿，不哀夭，不荣通，不丑穷。（《庄子·天地》）

　　楚威王仰慕庄子才学，欲聘其为相。他派人到濮水边，向正在垂钓的庄子发出邀请。庄子却头也不回，只是说："与其做死去留下龟壳让人们供奉的千年神龟，还不如让我自在地活在烂泥里，拖着尾巴慢慢爬。"在庄子看来，入朝为官无异于做一头祭祀用的牺牛，浑身披着织锦，享用精细的草粮，可等到一朝被牵入太庙受尽宰割，再想做回那头撒欢的小野牛，已是悔之晚矣。

　　Zhuangzi was fishing on the Pu River when the Duke of Chu who admired his talent and learning sent two high officials to see him, requesting him to administer the State of Chu. Zhuangzi went on fishing without turning his head and said, "I would rather be alive in the mud, happily wagging my tail than a died tortoise venerated in the duke's ancestral temple." To Zhuangzi, being an official in the court is just like being a sacrificial ox. Though it is draped well and fed well, once taken to the ancestral temple to be sacrificed, it will be too late to be that free and happy ox again.

◎惠子相梁图

A jealous and suspicious Huizi

惠施，战国时期宋国人，著名的政治家、辩客和哲学家，是名家思想的开山鼻祖和主要代表人物。

庄子虽然无意为官，却无法阻挡他人的忌惮与中伤。好友惠施（即惠子）当上魏国的相国后，庄子去探望他。惠子听信谗言，以为庄子是来夺取相位的，便命人在大梁城中搜捕庄子达三天三夜。

庄子听闻，主动去见惠子，说："南方有种鸟，名叫鹓鶵。它从南海飞往北海，不遇高洁的梧桐树从不栖止，不见竹实从不进食，不闻甘美清醇的泉水从不饮用。可笑的是，那专吃臭老鼠的猫头鹰，生怕鹓鶵夺食，发出声声恐吓。现在，你是要拿你的臭老鼠（魏国）来恐吓我吗？"

Zhuangzi had no intention to be an official, but that did not protect him from many spites and jealousies. His good friend Hui Shi, that is Huizi, was the Prime Minister of Wei State. Zhuangzi was on his way to visit Huizi. But Huizi believed the gossip he heard that Zhuangzi was coming to take his place to be the minister himself. So Huizi started a search all over the city of Daliang for three days and nights to find Zhuangzi.

Then Zhuangzi went to see him, and said, "In the south, there is a bird called Yuanchu. When it flies from the South Sea to the North Sea, it would not alight except on the Chinese parasol. It eats nothing but the fruit of the bamboo, and drinks nothing but the purest spring water. An owl which got a rotten rat, saw the bird fly by, and screeched. Are you not screeching at me with your rotten rat (the State of Wei)?"

漆园

◎蒙漆园吏图
Zhuangzi as an official

众人重利，廉士重名，贤士尚志，圣人贵精。（《庄子·刻意》）

对于朋友的猜忌，庄子一笑而过。而面对世俗的势利，他的讥讽则显得更为锐利。据《史记》记载，庄子曾出任漆园吏，但以他的孤傲与清高品格，为官自是不能长久。

Zhuangzi laughed off his friend's suspicion. His satire on snobbishness is so pungent. According to *Records of the Grand Historian*, Zhuangzi was once a small official, but Zhuangzi was so proud and aloof, pure and lofty that he did not keep the job for long.

癸巳暮秋冠心緩明钧於藏京弧竹古道居

◎庄子井

位于河南省商丘市民权县青莲寺村，相传为庄子生活取水处。

◎庄周借粮图

Zhuang Zhou borrowing grain

夫言非吹也。言者有言，其所言者特未定也。（《庄子·齐物论》）

平日里庄子身居陋巷，以编织草鞋为生，有时还饿得面容枯槁。一天，他不得已去向监河侯借粮，监河侯假惺惺地答道："行，我将要得到封地的税金，那时我借给你三百金，可以吗？"

Zhuangzi lived in a mean alley and made a living by making straw shoes. Sometimes he was so starved that he looked very tired and haggard. He went to an official who was in charge of irrigation works to borrow some grain. The official pretended to be very sympathetic to his situation and said, "No problem. I will loan you 300 *jin* (a weight unit in ancient China) of gold when I get the tax!"

◎涸辙之鲋图
A fish trapped in a dry rut

道隐于小成，言隐于荣华。（《庄子·齐物论》）

庄子当场拆穿了监河侯的虚伪，说道："我在来的路上，碰巧遇到有条鱼儿在车辙中呼救，它说自己是东海的水族，只想讨要升斗之水活命。而我答应它，将去南方游说吴越之王，引西江水来救它。那小鱼儿听后生气地说道：'现如今我失去了存身之所，只求一升一斗立时活命的水源，您可倒好，还要千里请水，竟不如早些去干鱼铺子找我罢了！'"

Zhuangzi exposed the official's hypocrisy right away and said, "On my way here, I saw a fish in the rut screaming for help, saying that it was from the East Sea and only asked for a small bucket of water to survive. I promised that I would go to the South to plead the king there to divert some water of Xijiang River to save its life. Hearing this, the fish flew into rage and said, 'I'm dying now, and only a small bucket of water can save my life. You go all the troubles to get water from afar instead. You'd better look for me in the shop for the dried fish!'"

◎巧讽曹商图
Zhuangzi scoffing at Cao Shang

不为轩冕肆志，不为穷约趋俗。（《庄子·缮性》）

　　宋国有个势利小人叫曹商，曾奉命出使秦国，得了秦王赏赐的一百乘车，回来见到住在陋巷中的庄子，便忍不住开口嘲笑他的贫穷困苦。曹商得意地说道："庄先生，要说住着小巷，织鞋糊口，饿得发晕，我不如你。可要说愉悦秦王，让他一次赏赐百乘车，恐怕这样的本事你就比不得我喽！"庄子也不辩白，只答道："秦王病中召医，破除其脓疮的人可得车一乘，舐治其痔疮的人可得车五乘。医治的方式越卑下，获得的车乘赏赐越多。看您这获赏百乘车的架势，想必秦王的痔疮都让您给舐治好了吧！"

　　In the State of Song, there was a snob named Cao Shang, who went on a mission to the State of Qin and was rewarded a hundred carriages when he returned. Seeing Zhuangzi still living in the mean alley, he derided his poor life. Cao Shang said smugly, "When it comes to living in a small alley, making straw shoes for a living and being starved to death, I'm not as good as you. But when it comes to pleasing the duke and getting the reward of one hundred carriages, you cannot do better than me!" Zhuangzi did not make excuse for himself, but just said, "The duke summoned anyone who could treat his abscess. Piercing the abscess, one can get a carriage; licking it, five carriages. The more degrading the treatment is, and the more carriages one can get. Look at the hundred carriages you've got, you must have licked them all!"

◎庄子见文王图
Zhuangzi meeting Duke Wen

人莫鉴于流水而鉴于止水，唯止能止众止。（《庄子·德充符》）

　　赵文王喜欢剑术，剑士们纷纷前来在他面前献技，相互拼杀，死伤众多。同时，尚剑之风也导致赵国游手好闲之徒日众，国力渐衰。太子为此忧虑不已，便以千金请庄子前来劝谏文王。庄子拒辞千金，慨然答应。他穿着剑士的服装，见了文王也不下拜，只说："我的剑，十步就可杀人，行走千里也无人能够阻挡。"

　　Duke Wen of Zhao liked fencing, which attracted a great many swordsmen.They attacked each other in front of the duke,with a lot of blood spilled.At the same time,more loafers appeared in Zhao state,so the strength of the state gradually declined.The crown prince was so worried about this that he pled Zhuangzi to persuade Duke Wen with rich reward. Zhuangzi refused to accept rich reward but paid the duke a visit. Zhuangzi was in his sword uniform and did not kneel down. He told Duke Wen, "I could kill a person within ten steps; I could travel a thousand *li* with a sword in my hand and no one can stop me."

◎庄子论剑图
Zhuangzi on swords

小惑易方，大惑易性。（《庄子·骈拇》）

赵文王听闻，十分欢喜，称赞庄子："您的剑法真是天下无敌了！"接着还宣召全国剑术比试中的佼佼者来和庄子比拼。庄子并不急于上场，而是对赵文王说："我拥有三种剑，您挑选其一。第一种是天子剑，它把燕溪的石城山当剑锋，齐国的泰山当剑刃，晋国和卫国当剑脊，周王畿和宋国当剑环，韩国和魏国当剑柄，用中原以外的四境来包扎，用四季来围裹，用渤海来缠绕，用恒山来做系带。运用天子剑，可开天辟地，所向披靡，匡正诸侯，天下顺服。第二种是诸侯剑，它把智勇者当剑锋，清廉者当剑刃，贤良者当剑脊，忠诚者当剑环，英雄豪杰当剑把。运用诸侯剑，能使海内臣民听从君主的号令。第三种是庶人剑，使剑的人蓬头乱发，瞪红了眼，拿性命互相激斗，对于天下却毫无用处。大王您现在就是处天子之位却爱好庶人之剑。"听完庄子的话，赵文王开始勤理朝政，不再玩物丧志了。

Duke Wen of Zhao was very pleased to hear that and said, "Your swordsmanship has no one to match!" And then he summoned all the winners in the sword contests to compete against Zhuangzi. Zhuangzi did not start the contest immediately, but said instead, "I have three swords, and you can pick one. The first sword is meant to be used by kings. This king's sword will help you to create a new world, conquer enemies, punish bad dukes, and the whole world is subject to you. The second sword is meant for dukes. The duke's sword will make the subjects listen to their kings. The third sword is to be used by common people. When they have swords in hand, they go into fight. They would stare at each other with their blood-shot eyes under their unkempt hair, risking their lives to kill each other. Their fights do no good to the world. Now though you are meant to be a ruler, your love for the sword is that of common people's." Hearing this, Duke Wen of Zhao no longer indulged himself in the meaningless contests, and started to pay serious attention to the state affairs ever since.

◎虎狼之仁图
Zhuangzi on benevolence

夫大道不称，大辩不言，大仁不仁，大廉不谦，大勇不忮。（《庄子·齐物论》）

宋国的太宰荡向庄子请教仁爱的问题，庄子答道："虎和狼也具有仁爱。"比起人类，庄子更愿意相信那些看起来凶残却从不伪饰的猛兽有着相互亲爱的仁德。太宰荡又问："什么是至仁?"庄子答道："至仁就是没有亲疏的差别。"普通的仁，是推己及人，是老吾老以及人之老，是己所不欲，勿施于人；而庄子的仁，则是放弃以自我为中心的大爱。

Minister Dang of Song State consulted Zhuangzi about "benevolence". Zhuangzi said, "Tigers and wolves also have benevolence." Compared with human beings, Zhuangzi preferred to believe the benevolence of those ferocious-looking beasts. Minister Dang then asked, "What is the ultimate benevolence?" Zhuangzi answered, "The ultimate benevolence is to love without distinction." The common type of benevolence is being considerate, expanding the respect of the aged in one's family to that of other families, and not imposing what you don't want on others. But to Zhuangzi, the ultimate benevolence is selfless love.

◎朝三暮四图
Fickle monkeys

朝三暮四，原比喻聪明的人善于使用手段，愚笨的人不善于辨别事情，后来形容反复无常。

庄子所处的时代，游士、学者都热衷于伸张自家学说，个个自以为登峰造极，当为天下所追崇。庄子却冷眼旁观，哀叹真正的道术已在无休止的争辩中分崩离析。庄子讲了这样一个故事："从前有位养猴的老翁，在给猴子分橡栗时提出：早上给三个，晚上给四个。猴子们都发怒了。老翁于是改口：那就早上给四个，晚上给三个吧。猴子们又喜形于色，却不知三与四的总和从未改变过。"在庄子看来，是非、美丑、善恶……这些表面的对立全都包容于完满的大道之中。而天下人却分门别派,辩论无休,劳思伤神,这和那些朝三暮四、忽喜忽怒的猴子没有区别。

Zhuangzi lived in an era when most scholars were eager to advocate their own thoughts and ideas. Each of them thought he already reached the peak of perfection, and deserved to be admired and followed. Zhuangzi told such a story: "There was a monkey-keeper who was in charge of the diet of acorns. He gave three in the morning and four at night to each monkey. The monkeys were all angry about this. The keeper said, 'Very well, then, you can have four in the morning and three at night.' The monkeys were all pleased, not knowing that there was actually no change." To Zhuangzi, the seemingly contrasting elements such as the right and wrong, beauty and ugliness, the good and evil all make harmony. But there are some people preferring to make the surface distinctions and trigger the endless and meaningless debates about the right and wrong. They are no different from those fickle and moody monkeys.

◎沉鱼落雁图
Zhuangzi on beauty

臭腐复化为神奇，神奇复化为臭腐。故曰："通天下一气耳。"（《庄子·知北游》）

"沉鱼落雁"的典故原本出自《庄子·齐物论》，后来人们常用这个词来形容女子的美貌。但庄子的原意却是这样的："人们眼中的美女，当鱼儿看见时就潜入水底，鸟儿看见时就飞到高空，麋鹿看见时就赶紧逃跑。它们不辨美丑，只是因为害怕而躲开。"人又何必用自己对美的定义来臆测其他生命的感受呢？

The allusion of "fish diving deep into the water"and "birds falling from the air" originally comes from *On Leveling All Things*, later people often use it to describe the breathtaking beauties. Nevertheless, Zhuangzi explicated, "In the eyes of people,some women were very beautiful.But when seeing them,the fish plunged deep into the water,the birds flew into the high sky, and the elks ran away immediately.They could not distinguish beauty from ugliness, but just escaped because of fear." How could we force our definition of beauty upon other creatures?

◎物之所同图
Zhuangzi on criterions

彼亦一是非，此亦一是非。（《庄子·齐物论》）

人住在湿地会腰酸背痛、疾病缠身，泥鳅却不会；人住在树上会害怕，猿猴却不会。庄子以人、猿猴、泥鳅的不同，来说明天下辩士整日争论不休的仁义、是非，其实也是千头万绪，一人一个标准，根本没有准绳可依。

If a man sleeps in damp places, his waist will hurt and back will ache. But this is not a case with a loach. If a man stays up in a tree, he will get frightened. But this is not a case with a monkey. Zhuangzi used this analogy to illustrate the differences among man, monkey and loach, and to show that it is pointless to argue over the right and wrong, the good and evil, since there is not a single criterion to go by.

癸巳暮秋冠心双眼翁松
盧東孤竹古蓬居

◎骊姬忧思图
The depressed Liji

梦饮酒者，旦而哭泣；梦哭泣者，旦而田猎。（《庄子·齐物论》）

在《庄子·齐物论》篇，庄子用骊姬的故事来比喻人们对于死亡的无端排斥："骊姬原是骊戎国君的女儿，刚被纳入晋国王宫时，思乡的苦楚与对未来的担忧让她整日以泪洗面。可是有朝一日，当她赢得晋献公的万千宠爱，每日与君主相伴，享用着各种山珍海味、绫罗绸缎时，骊姬不禁为过去的无知与眼泪而懊恼。"在庄子看来，死去后，人们或许也会为自己之前对死亡无谓的担忧而懊恼呢！

In *On Leveling All Things*, Zhuangzi told a story about Liji to explain people's rejection of death was actually groundless. Liji was from Lirong State. When she was captured and made an imperial concubine of the State of Jin, her tears rained down and drenched her coat. But after she had shared the duke's luxurious bed, fed on rich food, and draped in silk, she repented of her tears. In Zhuangzi's opinion, the dead might repent of their original worry about death!

◎鼓盆而歌图（一）
Singing for death（1）

夫哀莫大于心死，而身灭亦次之。（《庄子·田子方》）

　　庄子明白，生与死只是生命的不同状态，就好像是非、善恶、美丑只是事物的两面，都不是绝对的，因而无须为之过悲过喜。庄子的妻子过世，好友惠子前去吊唁，却见庄子在灵堂里叉开双腿，箕踞而坐，边敲瓦盆边唱歌，俨然一副事不关己的模样。看似离奇的"鼓盆而歌"的故事，最能体现庄子面临生死之变时的达观与超然。

　　Zhuangzi understood that life and death are just two different states. They are the two sides of things like the right and wrong, the good and evil, beauty and ugliness, and they are not absolute. So it is unnecessary to feel over-grieved or overjoyed. Zhuangzi's wife passed away. His friend Huizi went to pay his last respects, but only to find Zhuangzi sitting there with his leg crossed. He was singing while beating the earthen pot as if he were indifferent to her death. This "singing scene" seems unreasonable, but it actually shows Zhuangzi's detached view about life and death.

◎鼓盆而歌图（二）
Singing for death（2）

方生方死，方死方生；方可方不可，方不可方可。（《庄子·齐物论》）

  庄子鼓盆而歌，这让准备了一肚子安慰话的惠子瞠目结舌。惠子忍不住质问庄子："你们夫妇共同生活这么多年，她为你养育孩子，操持家务，守贫度日，辛苦如斯。现在她去世了，你不哭也罢，居然还鼓盆而歌，未免太过分了吧！"

  Huizi was lost for words at the sight of Zhuangzi singing while beating the pot. Huizi could not help questioning him, "You two have been living together for so many years. She raised your children, managed the household, and worked so hard for the family. Now she passed away, but you did not shed a drop of tear, and you even sang songs. That's too much!"

◎人故无情图
Zhuangzi on life and death

安时而处顺，哀乐不能入也。（《庄子·养生主》）

庄子答道："她这一走，我何尝真的无动于衷？又何尝没有落过悲伤的泪水？但细细想来，从前我身旁不也没有她执手相伴？从前这世上不也一样没有她这个生命，没有她美好的形体与灵魂？所有的生命，包括我和我的妻子在内，都是慢慢从'无'到'有'，由一片混沌隐约的气息化出具体的形骸与生命，之后再经由死亡重新回归到清净安宁的'无'。这样看来，人世间的变幻起灭与春夏秋冬的四季轮回又有什么差别呢？当亲爱的人终于平静地将自己的生命交还给运息交替的宇宙，我又凭什么非得在这里落一些无谓的眼泪呢？"庄子认为，人的容貌是大道所赋予的，人的形体是天理所给予的，人原本是无情的。这里所谓的"无情"，就是对于生死要顺从，对于荣辱得失也同样要顺其自然。

Zhuangzi answered, "How could I be so heartless over her death? How is it possible that I did not shed tears for her? But on the second thought, had I been with anyone before her company? Did her life, her beautiful body and soul ever exist in the past? All lives, including mine and my wife's, develop from 'nothing' to 'something', from the thin air into a form and life, and then go back to the tranquil 'nothingness' through death. Is there any difference between life and death and the change of seasons? When my beloved one gave herself back to the universe, why should I shed meaningless tears here?" Zhuangzi advocated "being heartless" of human essentially. The so-called "heartless" means accepting whatever life has to offer: glories one gets and the losses one suffers.

◎安知鱼之乐图
The fish's happiness

惠子曰："子非鱼，安知鱼之乐？"庄子曰："子非我，安知我不知鱼之乐？"（《庄子·秋水》）

　　有一天，庄子和惠子一道在濠水的桥上游玩。庄子看着水中自在摆尾的小鱼儿，不由赞叹道："鱼儿真是快乐！"爱好探究万物的惠子则在一旁问道："你又不是鱼，怎知鱼儿很快乐？"

　　庄子知道老友的脾气，偏要逗他一逗，又反问："你又不是我，怎知我不知鱼很快乐呢？"惠子一急，便道："我虽不是你，不知你知不知鱼儿快乐不快乐；但由此说来，你也不是鱼儿，又怎知鱼儿很快乐呢？"庄子微微一笑："我怎么知道的？我是在濠水的桥上知道的啊！"说罢便自顾自地逗弄水中的鱼儿去了。

　　Zhuangzi and Huizi strolled on the bridge over Hao River. When Zhuangzi saw a fish darting about in the water, he said, "How happy the fish is!" "You are not the fish," said the curious Huizi, "how can you know the happiness of the fish?"

　　Knowing him very well, Zhuangzi decided to tease him, "And you are not me, how can you know that I do not know?" "If I, not being you, cannot know what you know," urged Huizi, "it follows that you, not being a fish, cannot know the happiness of the fish." Zhuangzi smiled, "How did I know? I knew it by observing on the bridge." Saying that, he went on teasing the fish in the water.

◎大而无用图
Zhuangzi on uselessness

日出而作，日入而息，逍遥于天地之间而心意自得。（《庄子·让王》）

惠子指斥庄子的言谈荒诞无稽，就像不能盛水的大葫芦或是盘根错节的大樗树一样，"大而无用"，不能为世所用。但在庄子看来，同样的东西用在不同的地方，效果大不一样。人们要善于用发现的眼睛探索事物的最大价值，从而完美地利用它。自己的学说大有用处，只是惠子不能通晓领悟罢了。

Huizi criticized what Zhuangzi said as "big and useless" as a big gourd unsuitable for holding water, or a big tree with knobby trunk unsuitable for building materials. There was indeed no purpose for being too big to be utilized. To Zhuangzi, the same thing, used in different ways, has different effects. We should explore the maximum value of the thing with keen eyes so as to use it perfectly. His theories are of great use, but Huizi could not understand.

◎不龟手之药图
Salve healing chapped hands

不以物挫志。(《庄子·天地》)

庄子说:"宋国有人善于制造不龟裂手的药物,世世代代以漂洗丝絮为业。一日有客从远方来,出资百金买了他们的药方,并用此药方协助吴国在冬天的水战中大败越人,获得了吴王的割地封赏。"

Zhuangzi said, "There was a man of Song State who possessed a salve which healed chapped hands. His family, one generation after another, had been washers of silk. A stranger coming from afar offered him heavy gold for it. The stranger, having obtained the salve, went to help the State of Wu whose soldiers had chapped hands in winter time, and defeated the army of Yue State in the battle on the water. For this he was rewarded with land and made a noble."

◎浮游四海图
Floating on the rivers and lakes

人皆知有用之用，而莫知无用之用也。（《庄子·人间世》）

　　庄子感慨地说："同样是不龟裂手的药物，有人靠它漂洗丝絮，有人却用它赢得战争与封赏。由此可见，对于同一事物，就看人们如何去用。看似无用的大葫芦，为何不能系在腰间浮游四海？看似无用的大树，却正能因此保全自身而不受砍伐，人们还能寝卧其下。"

　　Zhuangzi commented, "For the same salve to heal chapped hands, it is important to the family who live by washing silk, but to another it meant the victory of a battle and a title of nobility. The differences lay in the way of using the same thing. Why cannot you consider the seemingly useless gourd as a huge cup in which you could float on the rivers and lakes? For the big tree, it is its seeming uselessness that saves it from being cut down, and people can still doze off in its shade."

癸巳暮秋冠心双明钧枉盛京
狐竹古道居

◎以此不材图
Unpredictable dilemma

真者，精诚之至也。不精不诚，不能动人。（《庄子·渔父》）

　　庄子认为，人们都知道有用的用途，却不知道无用的用途。"无用之用"，才是最大的用处。但也不尽然。在带领弟子游历天下时，庄子曾亲眼见过大树因为材质不良而躲过伐木者的砍伐，家禽却因为不会鸣叫而提早被主人宰割，有用者不能尽享天年，无用者也难逃一劫。面对不可预知的未来，面对生活中普遍存在的两难抉择，庄子说："那我就在有用与无用之间安放自己吧，虽然这也未见得圆满。"

　　Zhuangzi believed, people only knew the use of usefullness, but knew nothing about the purpose of uselessness. The usefulness of uselessness, is the largest. But it doesn't have to be. In his traveling with his disciples, Zhuangzi saw big trees escape from the trouble of being cut down simply because it was not good enough, but the cock get killed simply because it could not crow. The useful is not always blessed with what it deserves, and the useless also risks losing its life. Life is an unpredictable dilemma. For this, Zhuangzi said, "I might just as well place myself in somewhere between usefulness and uselessness, though it is not so ideal and perfect."

◎运斤成风图
A story about a craftsman

运斤成风，形容手法熟练，技艺高超。

惠子一生以口才自负，尤其喜欢与庄子争辩是非。他们虽然观点常有不同，但话语间机锋不断、妙语迭出，关系倒也非比寻常。惠子死后，庄子同样没有痛哭流涕，只是在惠子墓前看似随意地讲了个故事："楚都郢城有位粉刷匠不小心在鼻尖沾上了苍蝇翅膀大小的一块白土，让身旁一个叫石的匠人帮忙去掉。匠人石看也不看，抡起斧子就向他挥来，只听呼呼一阵风响，斧子过处白土转瞬无踪，那人的鼻子却毫无损伤。宋元君听说了这一奇闻，就派人把匠人石召进宫，让他也用斧子来砍自己鼻子上的白土。匠人石怅然道：'我过去是能这么抡斧子，但那个能和我一起完成这种默契举动的知己已经故去很久了……'"

Huizi was very conceited about his eloquence, and he really enjoyed arguing with Zhuangzi. Their witty arguments made their relationship quite close. When Huizi died, Zhuangzi did not cry either. He told a story in front of Huizi's tomb:"A painter from the State of Chu had a fine coat of chalk on his nose when he was working. He asked a craftsman whose name was Shi to wipe it. The craftsman swung his axe without a glance, and after a swooshing sound, the chalk was gone but the nose remained intact. When a duke heard this, he summoned the craftsman to the court, and asked him to wipe the chalk on his nose. The craftsman said sadly, 'I dared to swing my axe that way, but the one I had tacit understanding with and allowed me to perform that stunt passed away long time ago...'"

◎庄子思惠子图
Fond memories about Huizi

*君子之交淡若水，小人之交甘若醴。君子淡以亲，小人甘以
绝。*（《庄子·山木》）

　　讲完故事，庄子凝视着惠施的墓碑，幽幽地说道：
"自从你死去后，再也没有可以和我对话的人了，我也
不知道还有什么可说的了。"高山流水，弦断人亡，在
荒芜人世失却至交的创痛，本不是几滴眼泪所能表达
的。

　　Zhuangzi gazed at the tomb and finished his story sadly, "I
will have no one to argue with and nothing to argue about since
you died." It is difficult for one to find a soul-mate who could
appreciate the same piece of music, and it is not possible for one
to play the music with a broken string if his soul-mate dies. So
a few drops of tears could not express the grief one feels for the
loss of his soul-mate.

◎庖丁解牛图
Cook Ding dismembering an ox

游刃有余：厨师把整个的牛分割成块，技术熟练，刀子在牛的骨头缝里自由移动着，没有一点儿阻碍。后来形容做事熟练，轻而易举。

庄子特别爱用寓言来传达心中所想。在"庖丁解牛"的寓言中，庄子说道："庖丁有着非凡的宰牛技艺，他熟知牛的身体构造，将刀游走在牛筋骨间的空隙处，牛就像散落的泥块般豁然解体。整个宰牛过程自然流畅，令旁观者赏心悦目。普通厨师直接用刀去砍牛的骨头，刀一月一换；好厨师用刀去割牛的筋肉，刀一年一换；而庖丁的一把刀用了十九年，宰过数千头牛，刀口照样锋利簇新，关键就在于他懂得'游刃有余'。"在战乱动荡的年代，庄子既不追求过分张扬的"有用"，也不萎靡到彻底的"无用"。天道宏阔，人世的道路却狭窄如牛筋骨间的空隙，如何安身立命，实现"游刃有余"，应当不只是庖丁一个人的追求。"庖丁解牛"，看似熟能生巧，但庄子本身并不看重这些表面的技能。他更推崇的，应当是"庖丁解牛"中"技进于道"的内蕴。

Zhuangzi preferred to tell fables to illustrate his point. In "Cook Ding dismembering an ox", Zhuangzi said, "Ding had the skilled and magical craftsmanship in dismembering an ox. He knew the body structure of ox so well that he put the knife into the thin space between the joints, and wherever his knife went, the flesh came off, and the bones separated all perfectly in time. The entire process was very smooth and caused no discomfort. A general cook gets a new chopper every month, and this is because he hacks. A good cook gets a new chopper every year, and this is because he cuts. But Ding's chopper had been in use for nineteen years, and its edge was as sharp as it was new even after having cutting up several thousand oxen. The key was that he knew how to handle his knife with skill and ease." In a turbulent era when wars broke out frequently, Zhuangzi encouraged neither too much pursuit for "usefulness" nor reducing oneself to "uselessness". The road to heaven may be broad, but the road in our life is as thin as the space between joints. How to survive and establish oneself in the world is what everyone wants to achieve. "Cook Ding dismembering an ox" seems to teach a lesson of "Practice makes perfect", but this is not what Zhuangzi emphasized. He urged more of the way implied in Cook Ding's story rather than craftsmanship.

癸巳仲冬冠心望明钧拄盛京孙竹古道居

◎恶形美神图
The grotesque-looking beauty

形固可使如槁木，而心固可使如死灰乎？（《庄子·齐物论》）

谈到养生，人们一般想到的是食补、药补，或者通过加强锻炼提高身体素质。但庄子并不怎么关注外在形骸的健全与否，甚至在他的书中还常常会出现一些形貌怪异的得道之人。《庄子·大宗师》中提及的子舆，病得腰弯背驼、内脏移位，面颊缩到肚脐，却仍然步履艰难地走到井边，欣赏自己的倒影，赞叹造物者把自己变做曲背的人。子舆甚至还说："造物者要是将我的左臂变成公鸡，我就用它来报晓；要是把我的右臂变成弹弓，我就拿它来打鸮鸟烤肉吃；要是把我的尾骨变成车轮，把我的精神变成骏马，我就坐上它四处遨游！"在庄子看来，只要内在的德性高超过人，外在形躯是否完整、美好、健全就变得无所谓了。庄子还主张，人应当安时处顺，接受造化赋予形貌的一切变化。

When it comes to regimen, people often discuss a special plan of food, medicine, exercise etc. But Zhuangzi did not care too much about the completeness of one's physical body. There are some grotesque-looking characters in his writing. In *Masters in Zhuangzi,* there is a certain person called Ziyu. He was so sick that his back was all hunched up, his viscera all mis-located, and his cheeks down by his navel. Ziyu limped along to a well and looked at himself, gasping in admiration the Creator's job of making him such a hunch back. He said, "If my left arm were to be transformed into a cock, I should announce the arrival of dawn. If my right arm were transformed into a cross-bow, I should get broiled duck. If my buttocks were to be transformed into a wheel and my spirit into a horse, I should ride in my carriage." In Zhuangzi's opinion, for an honorable man with virtues, it does not matter at all whether or not he is healthy, complete or perfect in form. Zhuangzi also advocated that one should learn to be content with the good fortune and to be at home with the bad, and accept what is meant for his outward looks.

◎螳螂捕蝉，黄雀在后图（一）
The mantis stalks the cicada, unaware of the oriole behind (1)

至人之用心若镜，不将不迎，应而不藏，故能胜物而不伤。（《庄子·应帝王》）

一次，庄子到雕陵的栗林游玩 。南方飞来一只异常大的雀鸟，翅膀有七尺宽，眼睛有一寸圆，掠过庄子的额前。庄子拿起弹弓，快步追随，准备弹射这只奇异的雀鸟。

Zhuangzi strolled in a garden and saw an unusually big bird with long wings and big eyes flying over his head. Zhuangzi picked up the slingshot and followed immediately to shoot this strange bird.

◎螳螂捕蝉，黄雀在后图（二）

The mantis stalks the cicada, unaware of the oriole behind (2)

其耆欲深者，其天机浅。（《庄子·大宗师》）

　　这时候庄子看到，有只蝉正在树荫下独自休息，没有发现背后的螳螂正伺机捕杀它；而那只螳螂躲在树叶后蠢蠢欲动，并不知晓背后还有那只庄子准备弹射的大雀鸟预备对它下口。庄子见到此情此景，联想到天下万物相互牵累、相互招引，不由地扔下弹弓转头跑开，却被掌管山林的人当作偷栗子的贼，受到一顿责骂。庄子回到家中，整整三天都没缓过神来。

　　Just then Zhuangzi saw a cicada lying rest under a tree, totally unaware that a mantis was ready to catch it. The mantis who hid itself under a leaf did not know that the strange bird Zhuangzi wanted to shoot was about to catch it. Zhuangzi thought that everything in this world was inter-related and dropped the slingshot at this sight. But Zhuangzi was accused of stealing chestnuts and scolded by the garden-keeper. Zhuangzi went back home and was unable to get over the shock for days.

◎螳螂捕蝉，黄雀在后图（三）
The mantis stalks the cicada, unaware of the oriole
behind (3)

夫大块载我以形，劳我以生，佚我以老，息我以死。故善吾
生者，乃所以善吾死也。（《庄子·大宗师》）

　　弟子蔺且询问庄子为何如此不快，庄子将"螳螂
捕蝉，黄雀在后"的故事告诉他，并说道："我从前只
知道保养形躯，却不知道身体是有真性的，所以免不
了和那些螳螂、黄雀一般沉迷外物而迷失真性啊！"

　　Zhuangzi's disciple Lin Qie asked why he was so upset.
Zhuangzi told him what happened to the mantis, cicada, and
oriole. Zhuangzi then remarked, "I only knew how to take care
of my body, but not so much about my spiritual cultivation.So I
made the same mistakes as those mantis and cicadas — we were
all lost to external attractions!"

◎庄子著书立说图
Zhuangzi's writing

吾生也有涯，而知也无涯。以有涯随无涯，殆已！（《庄子·养生主》）

当其他诸子竭尽心力向天下推行自家学说的时候，庄子却从不曾将自己的言行视为天下的规则与典范。他坦诚地将自己的所见所闻告知读者，也将困惑与反思一一书写下来。庄子一边著书立说，一边思考着这些语言文字本身的意义。在他看来，语言文字当然有它存在的价值，但是世界上最好的意思却往往在这些语言文字之外。人们珍爱书籍，却往往迷失了更宝贵的"言外之意"。

When other thinkers tried every means to promote their thoughts and ideas to the world, Zhuangzi never tried to set what he said or what he did as the standard or model. He frankly shared with his readers what he saw, and what he gained from the things that confused him. Zhuangzi's writing focuses more on what is implied in the stories. In his opinion, words had their value, but ideas conveyed through these words were not in the words themselves. People loved their books, but they failed to understand "implications".

癸巳秋寒露寇心望明钺作於盧京孤竹古道居

◎轮扁斫轮图（一）
Wheelwright Bian on reading books (1)

言者，风波也；行者，实丧也。（《庄子·人间世》）

　　庄子用"轮扁斫轮"的寓言来解释何谓"言外之意"。齐桓公在殿堂上读古书，轮扁在殿堂下削砍木材，制作车轮。轮扁对齐桓公说："这些写书的圣人既然已经死了，那您读的不过是圣人留下的糟粕罢了！"

　　Zhuangzi illustrated "implications" with a story about Bian making a wheel with his axe. Duke Huan of Qi was reading classics in the court, while Bian was making a wheel down there. Bian said to Duke Huan, "The sages who wrote these books are all dead. What you are reading is just dross!"

癸巳仲冬冠心堂双明钤于盛京孤竹古道居

◎轮扁斫轮图（二）
Wheelwright Bian on reading books (2)

天地有大美而不言，四时有明法而不议，万物有成理而不说。（《庄子·知北游》）

　　齐桓公一听，生气地说道："做轮子的匠人怎么能随便议论圣贤的书？你要是讲不出道理来，就判处你死刑！"轮扁也不慌张，说："这是我从自身的经验中得出的道理。我对砍制车轮的奥妙得心应手，嘴里却表达不出来，连自己的儿子也教不会，到七十岁了还只能自己砍制轮子。"

　　Duke Huan of Qi was offended, and said, "How can a wheel-maker make such rude comments on the sages' books? If you cannot justify yourself, you will be sentenced to death!" Bian said in no hurry, "I've learned it from my personal experience. I know all the tricks and intricacies in making a wheel, but I'm unable to express myself and teach my son to do that well. As a result, I have to make wheels myself at the age of 70."

癸巳孟冬寓心斋明窗拈盛京孤竹古道居

◎轮扁斫轮图（三）
Wheelwright Bian on reading books (3)

无听之以耳而听之以心，无听之以心而听之以气。（《庄子·人间世》）

　　轮扁又说："写书的古圣人的生命，和他那些无法用语言表达的意思，早就烟消云散了，所以您读的当然也就只能是古人留下的糟粕了。"齐桓公不得不服，便饶了轮扁。

　　Bian continued to say, "The life of those sage authors was gone. So were the ideas they could not express in their words. Therefore, what you are reading now is the dross left." Duke Huan was convinced and spared Bian.

◎庄子论葬图
Zhuangzi on funeral

指穷于为薪，火传也，不知其尽也。（《庄子·养生主》）

当庄子走到生命的尽头时，弟子们纷纷表示要厚葬他，却被庄子一口拒绝。庄子说："天地就是棺椁，日月可做顶上的装饰，星辰可为陪葬的珠宝，飞禽走兽即是陪祭的食物，难道我的葬礼不样样齐备吗？"庄子从自然中来，又把生命交还给自然。他说过，人的生命虽然像燃料一样，总有燃尽的时刻，但人的思想与精神却像那些永恒不熄的火苗，总是带着光与热，代代相传。《庄子》一书，便是他留给我们的火焰。

When Zhuangzi was coming to the end of his life, his disciples wanted to give him a sumptuous funeral, but he refused flatly. He said, "The sky and the earth could be my coffin, the sun and the moon could be the ornaments, stars could be the jewels buried with me, birds and animals could be the sacrificial food for me. Don't I have everything ready to me?" Zhuangzi was born from nature and he wanted to return himself to nature. According to his thought, one's life was just like fuel which would not last forever, but one's spirit and thoughts were like flames carrying light and warmth and could be passed down to generations. The book *Zhuangzi* is what he passed down to us.

◎庄子墓

位于河南省商丘市民权县唐庄村东，现存墓冢高 2 米，面积约为 20 平方米，墓前有乾隆五十四年（1789）重修的庄子墓碑。

◎道去云天图
An immortal Zhuangzi

吾以天地为棺椁，以日月为连璧，星辰为珠玑，万物为赍送。（《庄子·列御寇》）

庄子的超凡智慧与飞扬文采，以及他不为荣华所惑、不受礼教束缚、愤世嫉俗却又嬉笑怒骂、隐逸而清高的人生姿态，对后世的司马迁、阮籍、嵇康、陶渊明、李白等都有着十分重要的影响。苏轼就曾坦言："读过《庄子》，才体会到自己一直没能说出口的那种千年的默契与感应。"《庄子》一书，对于魏晋时期的玄学清谈、南北朝时期的田园文学或志怪作品、盛唐时期的山水诗歌，以及明清时期的小说和戏曲创作，都产生了深远的影响。可以说，庄子为中华文明所渲染的瑰丽与奇妙的色彩，早已化入所有人的灵魂深处。

Zhuangzi's extraordinary wisdom and literary talent, and his refusal to be tempted by fortune and to be shackled by social restraints, his cynical attitude and detached outlook about life all deeply impressed writers and poets many generations after him. The famous poet Su Shi in Song Dynasty expressed his indebtedness to Zhuangzi, "I was unable to articulate the tacit understanding and connection until I read *Zhuangzi*." Zhuangzi exerted far-reaching impact on the literary styles in many dynasties. It is fair enough to say that the splendid colors Zhuangzi added to Chinese civilization has already entered into our consciousness.

跋

庄子，战国时之哲学家也。师法老聃，以道为本，所著《南华真经》存世三十三篇，分为内外二帙，多所寓言，抉幽入微、寄理其中。吾友明钧道兄近作四十图缀于文间，尽彰奥义，显著哲理。运生花之妙笔，赋缤纷之神采，若异鹊、梦蝶，挥洒恣肆、想象奇幻；如斫垩、解牛神态可掬、刻画入微，精采诸图未克备述，真乃适众口之脍炙，应誉画坛之新瑰。余得先睹，不亦乐乎，快览之余忝缀数语于后为跋。

甲午岁首于沈北
八十八叟老弘

Postscript

Zhuangzi is a philosopher during the Warring States Period. He studied under Laozi and upheld Taoism. His *Zhuangzi* consists of two parts of 33 articles, and most of them are fables full of messages. My friend Zhao Mingjun's 40 illustrations of Zhuangzi help to make the profound ideas easy to understand. Under his clever brush, the oriole preying on the mantis, the fluttering butterfly in Zhuangzi's dream, the cook dismembering an ox and the stonemason swinging an axe are all vividly and imaginatively presented. I cannot name all his pieces, and they are appealing to all the readers. Mr. Zhao is truly a great talent. I have the honor to take a first glance at his work and write a few words here to express my excitement.

An eighty-eight old guy Laohong
The beginning of 2015 in Shenbei District of Shenyang

跋

庄子、战国时之哲学家也。师法
老聃，以道为本，所著南华真
经存古三十三篇，分为内外二
帙，多所寓言，抉幽入微，寄理其
中，言支明均道元近作四十幅
缀於文間，更彰奥义，题着哲理
迂生花之妙笔赋缤纷之神采
若吴鹃梦蝶挥洒恣肆想象奇
□□所□□□甲□□□□□

后记

中国国家主席习近平在谈及中华文化时，深刻地指出：「中华优秀传统文化已经成为中华民族的基因，植根在中国人内心，潜移默化影响着中国人的思想方式和行为方式。」厚重、灿烂的中华传统文化，如何借由一种生动、直观、亲切的方式走进读者，尤其是海外读者的阅读视野中，一直是文化界关注、思索的问题。当《诸子百家国风画传》丛书带着「传承、创新、中国风」的鲜明印迹从上海出发，正是希望由此探索向世界传播、普及中国优秀传统文化的新方式和新渠道。

上海，作为国际文化大都市，通过源源不断地推出文化交流精品，成为海外读者了解中国、感受中国的一扇精彩窗口。发源于上海的连环画艺术，则以其浓郁、独特的中国韵味深受国内外读者的欢迎。两年前，以传承、振兴中国连环画艺术为主旨的上海海派连环画中心甫一成立，即在上海市政府新闻办的指导、创意下，联合发起策划一套以国风连环画为载体、契合「读图时代」特点的《诸子百家国风画传》丛书，并得到了

国务院新闻办公室、中共上海市委宣传部的大力支持，以及山东、河南省政府新闻办和相关诸子故里的密切协作。

尤为可贵的是，国内著名画家郭德福、李维定、赵明钧、邵家声、忻秉勇为淋漓再现智者先贤而实地采风，遍览典籍，泼墨挥毫，探寻中国文化符号世界化表达的崭新方式。画家们数易其稿，精益求精，创作出让人耳目一新、形神兼备的诸子形象。「画传不仅选取诸子生平中最具典型意义的事件，还注意表现鲜有人关注的诸子日常生活。画传想让读者感知的不只是存在于文献、传说里的古之圣贤，更是身边熟悉亲切、可以答疑解惑的智者。

我们衷心希望，这套充满哲理智慧与中国艺术美质的丛书能够成为连接当代与中华传统的文化桥梁。希望中华文化的寻源之旅能让每一个中国人寻回精神归属，也让海外读者从另一蹊径了解中国文化之美。

《诸子百家国风画传》丛书编委会
二〇一四年九月

Afterword

President Xi Jinping made an insightful comment in his talking about Chinese culture, "The excellent traditional Chinese culture has become our genes deeply rooted in our heart, entered into and colored our patterns in thinking and behaving." How the rich and brilliant Chinese culture could be presented in a vivid, visual and approachable form to the readers, especially overseas readers, has always been the concern of the cultural circle. When *The Pictorial Biographies of Great Thinkers* series with its distinguishing features of "inheritance, originality, and Chinese style" is setting sail from Shanghai, it is hoped to be a new means and a new channel explored for spreading, popularizing the excellent Chinese culture.

As an international cultural metropolis, Shanghai has created continuously first-class cultural exchange project and become a window through which overseas readers get to know and understand China. The comic book painting art originated in Shanghai has always been well accepted by readers home and abroad for its rich and unique Chinese style. Two years ago, not long after Shanghai Comic Book Center established to inherit and revive the comic painting art, under the guidance of Information Office of Shanghai Municipality, the Center created a series of comic book — *The Pictorial Biographies of Great Thinkers* to appeal to the "visual era". This innovative project is supported by The State Council Information Office and Publicity Ministry of Shanghai Municipal committee of CPC, and this project is also a close cooperation between Information Office of Shandong Provincial People's Government, Information Office of Henan Provincial People's Government and Confucius hometown.

What made this series particularly valuable is the research work the artists did. To represent thoroughly and faithfully the great thinkers, Mr. Guo Defu, Mr. Zhao Mingjun, Mr. Shao Jiasheng and Mr. Xin Bingyong, not only read extensively the classics but also conducted field work. They tried different means of expression and revised numerous times for a better unity of appearance and spirit of the thinkers. The episodes in the pictorial biographies reveal both the milestone events great thinkers experienced and their daily life that usually went unnoticed. The great thinkers in the pictorial biographies are no longer legendary figure in the literature, but amiable saints we can approach with our problems for a solution.

We sincerely hope that this series rich in philosophical wisdom and Chinese aestheticism could bridge the contemporary China and its traditional culture. We also hope that the exploration of Chinese culture will give every Chinese a sense of spiritual belonging, and provide an alternative for overseas readers to get to know the beauty of Chinese culture.

Editing Committee of *The Pictorial Biographies of Great Thinkers*
September 2014